Joined-Up-Writing

A Collection of Writings
From The CLAN Moray Writers Group

ISBN: 978-1-910205-48-8
Copyright
Margot Henderson

Printed by
For The Right Reasons
60 Grant Street, Inverness, IV3 8BS
Tel: 01463 718844 or 07717457247

Introduction

CLAN Moray have been delighted to hold the Words for Well-being writing class for our clients in Elgin.
We understand the importance of sharing emotions and not bottling them up. Writing is an excellent way to do this.
Over the weeks that the writing group has been meeting the enthusiasm and productivity has amazed me, poems and stories have made me laugh while others have brought tears to my eyes; this booklet is a testimony to the imagination and life experiences of the group and shows their positive outlook in the face of cancer.

Tracy Sellar
Moray Area Co-ordinator

Acknowledgements

A big thank you

To Abbeyside Care Group
to all the staff and volunteers at CLAN
to Stewart, Kevin and Richard at For the Right Reasons

Foreword

The CLAN Moray Writing Group began in March 2014, initially as a 6 week taster course. By the end of the 6 weeks people were hooked and the group had really gelled. We have been writing for a year now, with a few breaks in between. I have been so impressed by the group's commitment to keep writing and meeting, even in my absence and the ways in which they support each other. I have been so struck by the volume and quality of people's writing that I wanted to share it. This collection is just a small selection of the writers' work. Many of the writers have written much longer pieces which we couldn't include here...so look out for some solo collections to come

I am sure you will be touched and inspired by these writings. They are a testament to the resilience and creativity of the writers and to the wonderful work that CLAN does

When the group came up with the title 'Joined Up Writing' it seemed to me a perfect name for the book in that it says something about the strength, confidence and companionship that a writing group can offer people, especially when they are going through difficult times. Writing can be a wonderful way of meeting ourselves and each other with deeper understanding and kindness.

Margot Henderson

Contents

Pam Cumming

A Moment In Time
I Am Disabled Not Handless
Its Time
The Guest House
Mirror Mirror
Memory Lane
Blue Days
Golden Days
Scotland
The Wheel of the Year

Mary Mainland

This Is My Medicine
Guesthouse
My Nose Bothers Me
Oh This Being Human
Happiness Is
Blue Lady
3 Pieces Written to Music

Gerry Smith

There Are Times
The One Thing Worse
A New Guy For Me

Jill Stewart

First Day At School
When Cancer Happens
CLAN
Primrose Bay
The Race of Life
Time

Christine Bagnell

I am recently widowed, my husband died suddenly and unexpectedly of cancer. As you can imagine, this was a blow that was very difficult to come to terms with.

Communication by writing would not be my first choice and I was apprehensive about joining the writing group. But I found the group comforting and supportive in my journey of recovery. So I would encourage you to give it a try.

Write About

Putin, Ukraine
Write about
Right and wrong
Write about
Justice and fairness
Write about
Sea and sky
Write about
Happy and sad
Write about
Fast and slow
Write about
This and that
Write about
How and why
Write about
You and me
Write about
Us.

This Is My Medicine

-the beautiful snowdrops in my garden
-family and friends telephoning
- nice food
- my ipad to browse when I can't sleep
- reading a good book
- making things
- being with people who make me laugh
- kicking up leaves in the autumn
- being out in my garden

What Gets My Goat

paying for plastic bags
when my internet connection goes down
being left on my own
cars not giving way when you are wanting to cross the road
jars and food wrappers that are difficult to open
people throwing rubbish in my garden
unsolicited telephone calls
high postal charges for "Highland" addresses

Oh This Being Human

Oh this being human, fragile pieces on the board of life,
Loving, living, accepting all that comes our way?
But being alone comes as a cold shadow at the door,
Now no one to touch or hold you close, just a cold empty space,
no words,
no warmth,
no smile,
no emotion,
just me alone in my empty house,
wishing for all the world that is wasn't so.

Scotland Is

Scotland is –
Not for me the high mountains of loneliness and solitude,
the views stretching for miles and miles
but more the lowland walks beside babbling brooks
and along leafy glens and barefoot walks
on the beautiful white sands.
Not for me the wide open spaces, give me the Burrell,
the drumming and excitement of the Edinburgh Festival
the hustle and bustle of the Buchanan Galleries,
the River Festivals on the Clyde.
Not for me the Haggis and the white puddings
but the Aberdeen Angus steaks
and the delicious Tayside raspberries.
Scotland is for me a land of contrasts
with something for us all to enjoy.

Cancer Came

Cancer came like a bolt out of the blue,
killing all our dreams of a future together.
Cancer came and changed our lives
from shared walks along the beach
to zimmer frame walks along the corridor.
Cancer came and took over our lives
from shared meals at the table to bedroom dining.
Cancer came and swallowed us whole,
like an eagle snatching up its prey,
no battle to fight, just a short journey to travel to the end.
Cancer came and took him away and now
I feel all alone without him.

Ron Billing

Myself.

Retired but not tired, sometimes
Rushed off my feet
Romantic - been run out of town
Running - but easily caught
Reflective - but wouldn't change a lot
Riding the crest of a wave
Roads to the horizon still draw me
Roaring the sports car flat out
Right on to the end, 80 not out.

What the **the Writing Group** means to me
First of all the amazing friendships we have created,
talking about anything and everything.
On being given a subject to write about
I find it just flows out of the pen,
not always making sense.
Listening to others tales,
being amazed at their imaginations
and abilities to tug the heartstrings.
Come and see what stories are hidden in **your** pen.

Write About

Where I am now and how did I get here.
Pure accident because it didn't start off
with any pre conceived direction.
Write about a rocky road leading to a grand horizon,
so good is the view that the rocky road is forgotten.
Write about the fun we had on the way,
being chased by lions and zebra.
Write about flying in the heat of the day
where the haze hides all.

I Like

The smell of pitch pine
Walking my little dog
The morning cup of tea
A good dram
Sailing and sailing
Driving a good sports car
A good book
Laughter
Family love
Solving a mechanical problem
Being in love
Meeting old friends
Being fit again

Being at CLAN

Being surrounded by like minded people
Being able to air mutual problems
Not being any worse than I am, trying to hold on to the now
Hoping I`ll always remember this happy time.

My Happiness

Pleasing my dear wife.
Fixing a problem successfully.
Laughing at some crazy act we did together.
Seeing her laugh in spite of her pain.
Watching my little dog's antics.
Contentment at the grandchildren's successes.
Pride in sailing a good boat.
A seedless grape.
A well tuned engine on full song.
Dancing flames in the fire
A barbeque with no midges.

Talking about CANCER!

A dear old friend now long gone had the same problem as I have
now, Prostate cancer. But it was never mentioned, he had
'problems with down below'. Recently my wife's niece died with
Breast cancer but again it was never mentioned except in a
backhand whisper.
What is most apparent to me is the openness at CLAN and the
opportunity given to folk to talk about their cancer. My friend
and our niece didn't have CLAN to lean on. I have and I am so
grateful that they are there for me.

Down Memory Lane

Memory lane is a long lane.
The older you get the longer the lane.
It can invoke pleasure or displeasure
But most often the pleasurable recollections
overwhelm the unpleasant ones
So it's easy to cast aside the bad bits
making the happy recollections seem sharper.
Thus it is easy to go down a moss and clover clad path
colour the past and bring warm pleasure
at the memories of days of happiness,
When the sun always shone, and there was no pain.

Personal Journeys with Cancer

You see in my case there was no pain, just a deterioration of
functions. An investigation said it was cancer but to me it was
just a word. The first real impact after being told was when I told
my wife. She cracked up, but I didn`t. Ignorance was bliss.
If I thought about it there was a dull pain down there
somewhere. I was sent off to Aberdeen and stayed at CLAN for
seven weeks of radiotherapy. The only side affects I felt was
being tired. But after treatment finished I was as fit as a flea.

Eight years later in 2013, things started to go pear shaped again.
This time it hit like a brick 'cos the damn thing had grown again.
Two operations in Gray', lots of visitors, beginning to think they
knew something I didn't. In the film about Douglas Bader he
heard someone whisper outside the ward ' there's a man dying in
there ' He angered himself into life again and I felt the same
way. So I didn't die, family all disappointed, no legacy yet.
Gradually, gradually getting stronger. Being strengthened by the
special association with the good folk of CLAN.

On Being Human

A dog is the only other animal subject to prostate cancer.
They get ill and they die, no drama, no tears except from us.
We have to go through all the drama, deeper meanings,
the unfairness, 'why me'.
If this is being human they can stuff it!

I Don't Need CLAN

A man is supposed to be the stronger of the species
Right? Wrong!
I'm so independent I won't use a bus
Never used anyone, too much of a rush

Lift that bale, tote that barge
Always the one who stays in charge
Out on the road aye working over
Just one more sale to keep us in clover

We're supposed to be strong
'till something goes wrong
All of a sudden life goes awry
Dependent on others to just stay alive

They say it is Cancer, how can it be
I only came in 'cos I just couldna pee
They re-bored the hole with a pipe coming out
Life in the fast lane is now up the spout

Now stuck at home under wife's feet
Is this it? as I'm having a greet
I potter away, playing with old cars
But not very active because of the scars

CLAN opening in Elgin, some news I did see
Now's my chance to help others like me
I wander in past declaring my hand
Open arms greet me and I've joined in the band

And so here we are months down the line
Wearing a badge on my chest,
just to remind me who I am
Talking to everyone and listening to more
To anyone brave enough to walk through the door.

Here there is peace, a haven no less
Feels as though at last I've been blessed
CLAN is a family at last I have found
'tis hoped that they will long be around

Mini-saga
(a story in 50 words)

The start of something...

I see a tent with a single light inside casting shadows on the
coarse canvas.
The scent of trodden grass overcomes the smell of the shared fish
supper in the greasy newspaper. Replete after their feast the
pair of runaways are bubbling over with plans for their future.

Rebel Without a Cause?

I took 'Pagus', my Alfa Spider for a run Roseisle, to cheer myself
up and to introduce him to his predecessor, 'The Duke'. After the
formal bits were over, I had a ride in my old car just for old times
sake and found it a lot faster than 'Pagus'. But not to worry, I
had a feeling my throttle pedal wasn't quite right so that can be
sorted come time. After a most pleasant cup of tea sat in Kate's
lovely garden, she loaded me up with eggs and a bunch of
beautiful roses for Mary.

Spinning away up the road I flicked on the super duper
quadrophonic sound system where I caught the beginning of
Elgar's Nimrod. Turned up full belt it is awesome. It lasted
almost to Elgin. I suddenly felt mischevious and put on a
favourite old CD of Bernstein playing Gershwin, turned it up to
full chat and drove through Elgin High St. Heads were turning
and even kids were ripping their headsets off wondering where
the beat was coming from. Hell, it felt good to be 79 year old
rebel

CLAN Cavalcade 31st July 2014

The TV weather forecast was dire, strong winds and rain all over the north-east. After all the bonnie days of wall-to-wall sunshine it looked like our CLAN Cavalcade was going to be a washout. But no, munching our way through delicious bacon butties, courtesy of Jim Royan the butcher, and coffee, the sun actually came out whilst we all posed for the P and J photographer. So suitably refreshed our little convoy of a wide selection of Classics set off bound for the first drive past at the CLAN drop-in-centre at Inverurie. The folks in Inveruruie must have been scratching heads with all these lovely cars coming at them from all directions, but our first stop at Thainstone saw us all come together, just as a shower started. The Alfa's hoods were instant but some of the others took a little longer. The Mustang was best though with his power hood. Aberdeen and Northern Marts kindly provided tea and sticky buns free gratis and for nothing. Lots of interest from Joe Public in our venture and it was gratifying seeing groups out waving to us. On to CLAN House in Aberdeen where there was a lovely reception from the volunteers with lots of photo calls and interviews. A free lunch was laid on for us and then a tour of the grand facility which now exists to provide help and support and accommodation for those undergoing treatment for Cancer. Now we could get a good look at our fellow travellers. Two Alfa Spiders, two MGs, a B and a C, two Morgans, a Morris Minor tourer, a Stag, a Swallow Doretti, a Reliant Tempest looking very cute, a Mustang, a Sunbeam Tiger, a BMW 2002, and various moderns including a Ford Fiesta, Audi A8, a Subaru, a Toyota? The service bus from Banchory to Ballater joined in at one stage too.

The departure from the CLAN centre was delightful too, the traffic on Westburn Rd stopped to let us out so it seemed that even Aberdeen motorists fell into the spirit of the occasion. Onto Stonehaven where lots of people were waving to us and we found the CLAN drop-in-centre with everyone out in force cheering us on, the same in Banchory. By this time my co-driver Tracy was in charge getting to know the Alfa. But the rain, which had been threatening, suddenly dropped upon us so it was hood up time again. In Ballater we met at the car-park and found the eatery. Some of us were dragged off to the drop-in-centre for another photo shoot and that's where Alfa's starter refused duty and we needed a push. The lovely meal over we gradually made our ways home in some of the heaviest rain I've ever driven in. But it didn't dampen the spirit of the day one little bit. I personally thought it was one of the best day's motoring I've had for years and I sincerely thank all those who took part and for the grand sum of sponsorship that was raised, which at the time of writing amounts to £2800 with more to come in. Do it all again next year? I certainly hope so as we have high hopes of getting the Royals involved. Wouldn't that be a feather in our cap!

Tony Cardwell

Born 1943, a good year for claret I'm told.
I have lived with cancer for 10 years now
and hope to manage a few more.
Parkinsons came to call 4 years ago and has stayed,
becoming a permanent feature.

The Writing Group

is a spur to get me to put down on paper
Thoughts and ideas and has given me encouragement
to write some poems and short stories. I would say to anyone
swithering, "Come on and give it a go"

CLAN,

Extended family,
a friendly face, a cup of tea,
and folk who volunteer and spend
their time with others near the end,
or listen with a manner kind
to friend or family left behind.

A quiet room to contemplate
a life, a death, karma, fate.
also a place to sit and chat
and talk of life and this and that.

Peace and calm come to the fore
these feelings when I'm through the door
These are what CLAN means to me
that friendly face, this cup of tea.

The Human Condition

Am I on my own?
Not with friends like these
They give me support
just by being there
A smile, a hug,
no words need be spoken
A look or a touch do for me

Write About

Write about the things I love, family and friends
Write about the things I hate, the rest of this line's blank
Write about my bike, its saddle, chain and pedals
Write about my Parkinson's that bloody annoying tremor
Write about the spring, warm sun, long days, the summer
Write about 'Big C' ten years now and counting
Write about keep going!

Home Is

Home was a semi in a Nottinghamshire coal-mining town
(with a bit of farming around the edges). The Dukeries!
Early years playing in the woods, chewing on bits of sugar beet;
infant school, primary, secondary modern, rock and roll, girls,
college, girls, two years of engineering. Royal Marines: new
home.

The Way It Was

Listening to Radio Luxembourg on an old wireless with a lead
acid battery; Mum black leading the hearth, Dad coming home
from work on his motorbike; me falling off a high stool and
splitting my head open on the kitchen sink. The front room, only
used on special occasions and for much of the year about the
coldest room in the house! Kitchen windows, in winter the
condensation would freeze leaving more ice inside than out. A
roaring fire in the kitchen grate, making toast against the hot
coals, a new gas cooker and eating bread and dripping with a
sprinkle of salt on it. Coming home from school on my bike in a
storm, soaked to the skin, passing out with a dose of the flu,
being tucked up in bed with the luxury of a fire lit in the
bedroom grate!

Cancer Came

Cancer came, there was no 'bolt from the blue' and no 'I wasn't
expecting that!' There had been too many tests, scans,
examinations and frowns from the various medics charged with
the testing, scanning and examining.
I guess the crunch came when I was told 'It's malignant', that
was the 'gut wrench'. Even though I was half expecting it the
immediate flash of 'How long have I got' came into my head.
Malignant, even the very word conjures up thoughts of a slimy
noxious creature lurking unwanted and unbidden inside me.
I want it cut out, I want it destroyed, that poison hiding like a
worm in a piece of fruit or a wasp's gall in an oak apple.

It Brought

It brought another twist in the tortuous bike trail through life,
or some dropped stitches in life's rich tapestry.
It brought worry for my family.
It brought an operation (closely followed by a second),
six weeks of radio therapy, some years of stability
then off we go again!
It brought comments from well-meaning friends,
"Well if you're going to get cancer that's the one to get".
I smile wryly and tell them
"Yeah, but I'd rather not have it at all"

It Says

It says "I'm still here, you've tried to cut me out, but I'm still
here, you've tried frying me with x-rays but I'm still here, you're
trying to starve what's left of me by killing my food with your
implants. You try with your life-style, diet and your positive
thinking, but deep down you know I'm still here! I may be under
control (Or so you think!).

What Gets My Goat

Politicians can't answer yes or no, they shout each other down,
if they move their lips they're telling lies
or am I just being cynical??
The rest of life I'm happy with, I feel I'm quite 'laid back'
There isn't much that gets my goat,
I like to stay 'relaxed'

Enjoyment Is

Enjoyment is springtime, longer days, sun, new life.
Enjoyment is meeting good friends, a glass (or two) of wine, a
good curry.
Enjoyment is a good bike ride whatever the weather, day or
night.
Enjoyment is being in a good place in my head!
Enjoyment is a book or film that leaves me feeling good.

My Medicine

My medicine is to ride my bike
along the narrow twisting trails
through the forest;
to see a squirrel, deer or badger.
or a walk along the beach.
To sit and watch the waves
and the view across the Firth,
or gaze at the moon and stars
on a still clear night.

Haiku

The story-teller
A weaver of dreams
Transport to magical lands

Stars, bright, sparkling
Blue, silver and gold
Like ice in the firmament

The story is told
The tale teller gone
Only a memory left

A snowflake, dendrite
Pointed perfection
Each is individual

A wall falls, young flower dies
Parents wracked with grief
The world still turns

A land in turmoil
Ukrainians dead
Mother Russia stirs the pot.

Mini-sagas

The Singer

She strummed her guitar humming as she played, fingers
picking out chords. She tried a few words not all making sense;
words tumbled about in her head. Making a chord change words
fell into place, the song was taking shape. A second instrument
joined in, a new song was born.

Care Home

An old man cried out in pain while another groaned and
mumbled constantly. The Care Assistant, inured to such goings
on ignored them in their loneliness.
A shift change, new staff, the young girl, a novice, heard the
sounds and was drawn to them. Granddad she cried, tears
streaming down.

The Guest House

Parkinson's arrived like the breeze
through the top most branches of a tree
fluttering the leaves
and making the twigs shudder.
He stayed.
He became agitated
making the branches tremble.
When he's resting he talks
of a long journey to come,
When he's stressed, cold or angry
he shakes to his roots
and says he will never leave.

Dr Parkinson

Parky's my name and your hand I would shake
Once you're mine I'll not set you free,
I'll make you ache and your whole body quake
and your senses I'll take just you see!
Like a thief in the night I'll creep and I'll steal,
take your mind if I choose, and I can!
Take your voice, sense of smell and the loss will be real
and without help you'll surely be stranded
but for a while you'll be able to take from the table
your wine and drink it left-handed.

When I Die

When I die as die I must
my body will become as dust.

No stone or monument I crave
standing o'er a grassy grave.

My dust, just scatter on the earth
perhaps some seedlings given birth

Will rise and be nourished by my dust
will thrive and to the light will thrust

Their tender shoots through loam and peat
to bring new life, a thing so sweet.

My soul, if such things there are
now unfettered wanders far.

Old friends who've gone before to find
a speck, a mote 'mongst all mankind.

In memories I may linger on
but from the earth my light has gone.

Pam Cumming

My name is Pam Cumming and I am a survivor of breast cancer. Between having MS and depression, my life is a daily challenge but I am thrawn and my motto in life is "Carry On Regardless"

When I left school, I could barely read. So when I joined the CLAN Writing Group I thought I would be hopeless. The teacher somehow manages to coach poems and stories out of us. The group has given me the confidence to write my first novel.

A Moment in Time

Each person needs
a few moments for themselves.

A time away
from our mundane chores
of everyday life,

To daydream of faraway places
and of deep fantasies,

A time to mull over
what has been said or done,

A time to reflect on bygone times
where hopes and dreams
come to life, or not.

Just a few moments,
that's all we need,
to recharge our batteries,
So we can face the world again.

I Am Disabled, Not Handless

My legs are not working so well,
but the rest of me is working fine.
From time to time
I need to go into my wheelchair,
to give my legs a rest.

I am more than capable
of getting my own coffee,
I have to do it at home.

Please stop and think for a moment,
before you rush to help.
My mouth works perfectly well.
so if I need help I will ask for it.

Put yourself in my shoes
or even my wheelchair.
Think how you would feel
with people fussing over you,
with pity in their eyes
I can tell you here and now,
you just won't like it
as I don't.

All I ask of you is to treat me
as you would want to be treated yourself.
Look past the wheelchair,
and see the person in it.

It's Time

It's time to walk the path to recovery,
Throw of the past and find new discoveries.

It's time to rise and stand tall,
To pull all my strength to give it my all

It's time to fill my heart with wonder,
New dreams can be sought over yonder.

It's time to take care of my mind, body and soul,
Food for thought and exercise new goals

It's time to look forward and think happy thoughts,
The past is the past, inner demons have been fought.

It's time to be strong and lock my fears away,
Nightmares are vanquished by the first light of the day.

Its time its time its time.

The Guest House

Loneliness comes to my door,
a shroud of mist encasing her.
I see her, she doesn't see me.

I talk to her, she looks up,
but all she hears is a whisper.
I reach out my hand to let her know I'm here.

But the mist around her
prevents me from touching her.
Loneliness turns away in tears,
not knowing someone was there.

Mirror Mirror

She stands looking into the mirror,
sadness in her eyes.
"Why?" she said, 'Why me?'
with tears rolling down her face.

"Why not you?" the mirror said.
She stood pondering, "Yes." she said,
"You are right. Why not me!
I know I'm stronger than I think.
I can do this."

Memory Lane

As I travel down memory lane,
what knowledge will I gain?
Times of pain and times of strife
but hey ho that's life.

Should we dwell on what we cannot change?
This is the present
the past cannot be exchanged.
To look forward to the future
we must learn from the past,
To forgive and accept, the notion is cast.
To live in the past and forget
to live in the now,

Future events will be lost and how.
So make plans for the future
and leave the past where it is.

Blue Days

There are some days when we just don't want to get out of bed,
But somehow we do.
There are some days when we just want to wear our jammies all day,
But somehow we manage to dress ourselves.
There are some days when nothing we do is right,
But somehow everything works out alright in the end.

There are days when everything we say is wrong,
But somehow everyone knows what we mean.
There are some days when we feel we are climbing a mountain,
But somehow we manage to climb down the other side.

There are some days when we just want to run and hide,
But somehow we manage to muster our strength to face the day.
Blue days we all have them,
But we all try to keep our chins up and smile and keep going.

Golden Days

There are some days we jump out of bed,
Just knowing it's going to be a great day.
There are some days we rush to get dressed,
Just to see what the new day brings.
There are some days we will try something new,
Just knowing it will work out fine.
There are some days our hearts feels light with joy,
Just knowing it is wonderful to be alive.
There are some days we can't help smiling at strangers,
Just to see if they smile back.
There are some days we make plans for our future,
Just hoping these plans will come true.
Golden days we all have the, even though they may be rare.
Just knowing when we have learnt to deal with the blue days,
makes the golden days even more special.

Scotland

You are a country where I call home.
You are a country steeped in history
from warrior Picts with painted faces
to ancient kings and queens.
You have beautiful scenic mountains and glens with winding roads.
You are the only country in the world where you can bag a Munro or two
and have all four seasons in a day or even in an afternoon.

In your land great battles were won and lost
like Bannockburn and Culloden.
Brave men women and children died on those days
but will never be forgotten.
In ancient times children would listen to stories told around open fires
about mythical beasts like kelpies and brounies or the tree fairy Ghillie Du.
and tales of the battle between Beira the queen of the Winter
and Bride the queen of the Summer.

In your land farmers will plant crops of oats, rye and barley
so we can make our porridge bread and whisky.
In their fields are roaming hairy highland cattle and Aberdeen Angus
soon to be the Sunday dinner.
Or for a midweek treat mothers may serve Cullen skink,
haggis, neeps and tatties and even clootie dumpling
and for a treat but only if we have been good some homemade tablet.

In this country great men and women have been born here
from doctors to inventors, entertainers and politicians
to the everyday person.
This country and the people in it may not always be perfect,
but it's the only country I want to live in, this is where I call home.

The Wheel of the Year

As the wheel of the year turns from season to season,
from birth growth life and death,

As the wheel turns to Spring it is a time of eternal hope and birth
planning for the garden, what vegetables will we grow?
Love in the air and Valentines cards; spring bulbs and new buds
growing on the trees; clocks going forward and lighter nights.

As the wheel turns to Summer it is a time of long hazy days
and summer breezes. Growing vegetables,
salad days; picnics and barbeques
Sea side jaunts and sandcastles; Druids gathering at Stonehenge
to greet the Summer Solstice at the longest day of the year.

As the wheel turns to Autumn it is a time of changing colours
of gold's and reds; gathering of conkers and fallen leaves
flying high in the autumn gales;
Darker nights and darker mornings;
scary costumes at Halloween
an extra hour in bed, the autumn harvest
and storing for long winter days

As the wheel turns to Winter it is a time
of cold hands and red noses.
Falling snow and icy roads, planes, trains and automobiles grounded
to a halt; the Winter Solstice and the longest night of the year;
Holly, mistletoe and Christmas Carols;
Father Christmas and his flying reindeers come for a visit.
Festive food and comfort food; hard times and shortages.

Death leads to rebirth

Mary Mainland

I was part of the original cancer group. Having had personal experience of cancer, I offered to help with any fundraising that was to be done. Having stayed in CLAN with my late husband and my present partner, I felt it was payback time for all the marvellous help that I had received.

Tuesday's Writing Group has been a lot of fun. I have learnt a lot, met new friends, found talent I did not know I had and got strength from my writing.
It helped to get rid of some memories by writing them down

CLAN gave me hope for better things.
A clearer mind, to understand cancer,
Help to move forward,
and, onward to better days.

This Is My Medicine

Being with friends.
Being with my granddaughter.
Cooking.
Helping others.
Not wasting energy on anger.
Retail therapy
Walking with the dog.
Watching the sea.
Working in the garden.
Watching a documentary.

Guesthouse

Illness came a knocking at my door
Illness came through my door
Illness has an ugly taste.

It spoils your food but trims your waist.
It spoils your taste buds they have up and gone.
Food for life is all you could say,
as you eat to live but don't really enjoy.

As time goes buy things do improve,
tasty treats help to sooth the heat.
But illness you are a horrid pill
so please leave me so I can be well again.

Mini Saga

My Nose Bothers Me

A sunny day I go to town for the messages.
Glory on, feeling fine, enjoying the breeze.
Then lo and behold a skip I see, and I have a peep.
The next I know the ground appears.
Laughing and sore,
that's what you get, when your nose is too big.

Oh This Being Human.

Oh this being human,
it can be hard to smile today.
Strength comes when it is needed
so stand up and fight.
It helps you keep going
and see a bright light.
We can sit down and cry
and we'll do it alone.
Or you can smile and get on.

Happiness Is.

Being well, content, helping others,
giving time, stop hurrying!
If you feel happy and smile
it can be infectious and help others,
It can brighten your and others' day.
Happiness is a state of mind
where you can go when feeling down to cheer you.
Being happy helps you keep healthy,
You work better, feel better and smile.

Blue Lady

I went to the garden party feeling sad and blue.

I had been asked to bring Bed Dolls-a decoration for your bed.
They were left over from a previous fundraiser.

Pam was doing her duty on the gate.

This same lady says sometimes she wears a false smile,
when she is blue.
But her heart is certainly not false.
She knew I was sad and feeling blue too.

Holding out her hand and with a big smile
she gave me a note with her phone number.
This is to help for when you are sad.
So call me to talk when you need help.

Then when it was over and I go to leave
Pam gives me a big hug

3 Pieces Written to Music

Soothing

Soothing, relaxing invigorating
full of life
I want to go to sleep
and the trials of life will fade away
So soothing and relaxing
you go with flow and fade away
When waking all is well
Life is good
and the trials have faded away

Hawiian Islands

Sun, sea, sand
Dancing in the dusk
after a lovely dinner of good food and wine
the end to perfect days
Seeing new places
and things to remember
when holidays are a distant memory
and the humdrum of life is with us again

A Night At The Opera

A night at the Opera with friends
to hear good music and song
with these beautiful singers.
with voices to die for
who make the scenes so vivid
they are real and most enjoyable
to watch and hear
leaving one refreshed
invigorated by it all

Gerry Smith

I initially found comfort and friendship at Clan, with great memories of my stay in the old building in Aberdeen.

Joining the writing group opened up another door to the trust and friendship that developed within that, particularly after each of our revelations that we were all able to share with one another.

These three pieces came straight from my heart one evening, as I said at the time, and have been very appropriate during my cancer time.

There Are Times

There are times
when I don't want to do this anymore,
Yet, something inside drives me on.

There are times
when I find it too hard to bear,
Yet, something inside drives me on.

My body defaced
but my heart still in place,

Whenever will there be
a new guy for me.

The One Thing Worse

The one thing on earth worse
than being alone
is being alone when together

With something that takes
all you were and you are
and changes your norm forever.

A New Guy For Me

Whenever will there be,
a new guy for me,

Someone who cares,
who sees not my scars.

My body defaced
but my heart still in place,

Whenever will there be
a new guy for me.

Jill Stewart

The CLAN Elgin writing group offered me the opportunity to engage with volunteers and clients alike, providing an invaluable source of support to all. We exchanged ideas, shared enjoyment in each other's work and fostered creative and personal skills as we read aloud our efforts to a trusted audience each week. Most importantly, we had fun and encouraged each other to "have a go".

First Day At School

I was excited to be a 'big girl' at last. My school bag and pencil case had been packed for weeks. Twelve shiny pencils all sharpened and ready for action.

I remember the scratchy starched collar of my school blouse unlike anything I'd ever worn before. The long walk to the school gate, squeezing my mother's hand tighter and tighter as the intimidating building with its high windows came into view. I began to trail my feet and walk slowly complaining of sore heels being rubbed by unattractive black lace up shoes.

Suddenly on turning a corner and hearing the cacophony of screaming, laughing children along with the jangling school bell I took fright. I tried in vain to convince my mother I was ill – crying about my collar choking me, my shoes hurting, something in my eye, sore tummy. My avoidance tactics were all unsuccessful and I found myself being ushered into a classroom with some forty other infants. The cloakroom smelt of disinfectant and the classroom was dark and dingy. To make matters worse, the teacher was reading 'Brer Rabbit's Tea Party'. I had that book at home and didn't need to hear the story again so I bolted for the door and ran all the way home.

When Cancer Happens

When cancer happens it happens to the whole family. It feels as if a whole team of people is under an unimaginable degree of stress, often for weeks or months at a time. Emotions run amok and it is difficult to preserve any degree of normality. The emotional rollercoaster is magnified by exhaustion, worry and fear. It can feel like the house has become a prison with lots of unwanted visitors but no-one leaving, and everyone inside walking on eggshells under a heavy blanket of sadness.

CLAN

The gift that CLAN has given me is to be able to sit with people who are troubled, to be there **with** them and **for** them. People who are afraid and isolated need someone there and I feel privileged that I get the chance to help them face whatever lies ahead. I enjoy bringing relief, presence, peace and companionship not only to the cancer sufferer but also to their family. It is particularly rewarding to work with children who are carrying the hurt of cancer around with them everywhere they go, to work with them and let them know that their feelings are normal, to reassure them that other boys and girls have felt the same way is extremely humbling. CLAN allows children to feel less alone during a very difficult time and helps them turn a corner towards a new kind of 'normal'.

CLAN is a team of people who are always there and will be there whenever they are needed. The level of support they provide brings comfort to a whole family and helps them on their unique journey through cancer along with their loved one. The passion shown by CLAN volunteers can't be manufactured. It takes strength to look cancer in the eye and still smile from the heart.

Primrose Bay

Primrose Bay - even the name suggests a lazy, picturesque holiday resort, but the area is surrounded by mystery and intrigue. Some twenty or thirty years ago the inhabitants of the cluster of pretty cottages on the cliff top were worried about their strange new neighbour. Even after all these years the locals still gossip and enjoy a yarn about old Harry Toms.

By day his cottage looked exactly like all the others except that, at every window, his curtains were kept tightly drawn and his garden remained wild and untidy. However, by night it was a completely different story when peculiar, eerie music could be heard and bright lights blazed from within the cottage. What was going on inside? Nobody knew.

On very rare occasions, the old recluse was spotted outdoors. He always wore a heavy black raincoat, huge clumpy black boots and a brown hat with a wide turned-down brim that hid his unshaven face. The residents of Primrose Cottages tried to befriend him and say 'hello' but whenever they approached he would quickly dart back inside and slam his front door. Children from the nearby school would dare each other to hide behind his overgrown, unkempt hedge and call out rude names in the hope that he would charge out in rage and chase them away, but he never did. The children were disappointed but kept trying as if it were a challenge. Only Maggie McIntosh, owner of the village shop, ever spoke to the old hermit on his once a week visit to buy a few tins of food. She gradually found out that his name was Harry Toms and that one day he hoped to become a millionaire.

Life in this sleepy little community went on uneventfully like this for a long time until suddenly, one morning everything changed. Old Harry's curtains and doors were open wide. What had happened in the night? News soon spread and the villagers came to look, although they were all too afraid to venture up his garden path. It was decided that the police should be called.

What a surprise awaited them. They discovered one tiny, humble bed-sit while all the other rooms were furnished like extravagant art galleries, hung with exquisite paintings. The secretive, solitary old man had been an artist trying to make his fortune.

There was never any sighting of Harry Toms and there still hasn't been till this day. Had he taken his finest, most outstanding painting with him to sell? No-one will ever know.

The Race of Life

"In the Race of Life, don't waste your energy and time trying to compete with others. Sometimes you are ahead, sometimes behind. The race is long and in the end, it is only with yourself . . . . . ."

With this in mind, I thought of how lucky I was being invited (or perhaps bullied) to join my daughter Rebecca and a host of her friends to power my way around the 5km course.

Let's face it, the weather has not been great recently, and while I would love to tell you that the event was bathed in glorious sunshine, it would be a bit of an exaggeration. But, and this might sound strange, I'm really glad it wasn't in the end. Sure, when I got out of the car wearing running gear (at my daughter's insistence) and was greeted by a wall of rain and wind, I did have some misgivings. However, from the moment I arrived at the event, those doubts just faded away.

While it's hard to explain in words, there was something quite magical about doing the Cancer Research warm up dances in a biting wind while the rain lashed down. It felt really empowering – a huge collective act of defiance against cancer. That no matter what **it,** or the weather throws at us, we will stand strong and battle through. The actual Race was the same. As we ran, walked and jogged round the course, friendly strangers came together, united against the elements and had a fantastic time.

Time

Time...
The infant's hand reaches from its cot
Tiny, grasping, outstretched to turn the hour-glass
To set the steady stream of sand in motion

Time...
Consistent, continuing, never-ending
All through life in a perpetual procession of minutes
There is no stopping, no interruption, no turning back the clock

Time...
Nearing the end, the stream flows slowly but...
The old wrinkled hand outstretched in vain,
Feebly tries to turn back time

But just as grains of sand slip through the hour-glass
The final minutes escape and are lost for ever.